Everyday Prayers for Teachers

EVERYDAY
PRAYERS
for
Teachers

DIMENSIONS
FOR LIVING

NASHVILLE

EVERYDAY PRAYERS FOR TEACHERS

94 95 96 97 98 99 00 01 02 — 10 9 8 7 6 5 4 3

This book is printed on recycled, acid-free paper.

ISBN 0-687-31695-2

The Steps of Prayer is adapted from HOW TO PRAY,
E. Stanley Jones. Copyright © 1943 by Whitmore &
Stone. Used by permission of Abingdon Press.

MANUFACTURED IN THE UNITED STATES OF AMERICA

Contents

The Steps of Prayer

First, decide what you really want. The "you" is important. It must not be a vagrant part of you wandering into the prayer hour with no intention of committing yourself to your prayer request. You cannot pray with a part of yourself and expect God to answer, for God hears what the whole of you is saying . . .

Second, decide whether the thing you want is a Christian thing. God has shown us in Christ what the divine character is like. God is Christ-like. He can only act in a Christ-like way. He cannot answer a prayer that would not fit in with his character . . .

Third, write it down. The writing of the prayer will probably help you in self-committal. For, if you write it, you will probably mean it. The writing of it will also save you from hazy indefiniteness . . . There will come a time, of course, when you may not need to write things down, for they will have written themselves in you . . .

Fourth, still the mind. The stilling of the mind is a step in receptivity. Prayer is pure receptivity in the first stage. "As many as received him, to them gave he power." If you come to God all tense, you can get little . . .

Now you are ready for the fifth step: Talk with God about it. "Talk with God," not "Talk to God," for it is a two-way conversation. And the most vital part may be, not what you will say to God, but what God will say to you . . .

There is a sixth step: . . . At this point be silent to hear God again, and see if he makes any suggestions to you about your part in answering the prayer. If definite suggestions come to you, then promise that you will carry them out . . .

Seventh: Do everything loving that comes to your mind about it! This step is important, for it is a cleansing and clarifying step. The word "loving" is important. The first fruit of the Spirit is "love," and if the suggestion does not fit in with love then don't do it.

Wait for the suggestion that does fit in.

Eighth: thank God for answering in his own way. God will answer that prayer. No prayers are unanswered. But God may answer "no" as well as "yes." "No" is an answer, and it may really be next in order leading on to a higher "yes."

There is a ninth step: Release the whole prayer from your conscious thinking. Don't keep the prayer at the center of your conscious thinking. It may become an anxiety-center. Let it drop down into the subconscious mind and let it work at that greater depth. Then there will be an undertone of prayer in all you do, but there will be no tense anxiety. Dismissing it from the conscious mind is an act of faith that, having committed it to God you leave it in his hands, believing he will do the best thing possible . . .

E. Stanley Jones

I Sit Down Alone

I sit down alone, only God is here;
In his presence I open, I read his books;
And what I thus learn, I teach.

John Wesley

The Good Teacher

The Lord is my teacher,
I shall not lose my way.

He leadeth me in the lowly paths of learn-
    ing,
He prepareth a lesson for me every day;
He bringeth me to the clear fountains of
    instruction,
Little by little he showeth me the beauty
    of truth.

The world is a great book that he hath
    written,
He turneth the leaves for me slowly;
They are all inscribed with images and
    letters,
He poureth light on the pictures and the
    words.

He taketh me by the hand to the hilltop
    of vision,

And my soul is glad when I perceive his
meaning;
In the valley also he walketh beside me,
In the dark places he whispereth to my
heart.

Even though my lesson be hard it is not
hopeless,
For the Lord is patient with his slow
scholar;
He will wait awhile for my weakness,
And help me to read the truth through
tears.

Henry Van Dyke

Morning Prayer

Dear God, I learned a prayer when I was in first grade. It was only four lines long, but I said it every day:

Good morning, dear God,
I offer to you
My thoughts, words, and actions
And all that I do. AMEN.

It's a simple prayer, but, lately I have tried to make myself remember it when I awake in the morning. I use it as a prayer starter and go on to add my own prayer to it. It inspires me to speak further and more deeply with you. The day has a much better beginning when it starts with you. I have a much better beginning when I start with you. AMEN.

For Insight

God,
One who knows me
better than I know myself . . .
and loves me with a steadfast love . . .
lead me this day to know you better.
Surprise me with new insights into your
    activity
in the world, so my students may know
    you as a God
who is involved in the world—
and in their world. AMEN.

Anonymous

For Effectiveness

Teach me your ways, Lord,
so that I may teach
with love,
with patience,
and with the knowledge
of your presence. AMEN.

Prayer Before Class

Dear Lord, may your spirit guide my teaching today. Help me to make the lesson come alive. Help me to present the material so that the interest sparked will grow with the years. Make me sensitive to my students—to their ideas and moods, that they may be free to ask questions and speak their thoughts. Help us to have a happy class period today. AMEN.

Friday Afternoon—After a Good Week

Dear Lord, this has been an exhilarating week. Somehow everything came together—the students, the subject, my own enthusiasm . . . and you were there too with us, guiding us, inspiring us.

Help us always to be aware of your presence with us. Let us praise you and thank you for your guidance—when it is easy to remember to do so, and especially when it is not so easy.

Thank you for days and weeks such as this one and for the strength and endurance they give us. And thank you for leading me to this profession. May all my efforts praise you. AMEN.

Before a Pep Rally

Here we go to the gym, Lord, for the first pep rally of the year. The kids are so excited, the cheerleaders so enthusiastic, the team so nervous. We're undefeated, we're number one.

But somehow, Lord, help us keep a perspective on this season and these games. These players started tossing balls when they were still toddling around because it was so much fun to be able to catch a ball and to throw it far enough for someone else to catch it too. Suddenly, the whole idea of winning seems to take over. Is it still fun just to play?

Help us all—not just the players and students, but parents and coaches and teachers too—remember to thank you for our health and our physical abilities, to offer our best efforts to you, and to enjoy playing the game. AMEN.

When a Student Has Died

This is a teacher's worst nightmare,
Lord. She woke with a terrific headache
three days ago. Then we heard about
spinal meningitis. Now she is with you.

Why? Why her? It is hard to let go and
accept what we cannot understand.

And the students are frightened and
their parents are frightened and we teachers are frightened. All of us who were with
her are on medication now. It distracts
us—did we begin our treatment in time to
arrest this virus?—it distracts us from our
grieving.

Lord, give us strength through these difficult days. Help us help one another. Be
with her family. Let our faith and love for
you keep us focused and steady. And let us
not forget to praise you for her life, and
thank you for the privilege of knowing her.
AMEN.

For Disciplining

Lord, it is difficult when I have to pun-ish the students. Sometimes I think it upsets me more than it bothers them. My prayer is for the ability to be consistent and fair.

When I think back to the teachers who inspired me and who first attracted me to this profession, I recognize the qualities in them that I wanted to emulate. The ones I admired most, I think, were the ones who were fair.

So, I am asking for your help again, Lord. Help me have the strength and integrity to know when a situation calls for patience and when it calls for discipline, and please help me when I try to discipline fairly so these students will learn not only from their mistakes, but also from my example. AMEN.

Before Christmas Break

I don't know who's more excited,
Lord—the students or me. I wonder if they
realize I am counting the days as much as
they are.

On these days, we ask for your assis-
tance. Help us concentrate on our work.
Help us concentrate on the meaning of
this season and on your birth. When my
mind wanders, it's not to the Christmas
story that it goes. Instead, it wanders
toward preparing the house for family and
friends, shopping, cooking, sending cards
to those far away. So I ask for the ability to
focus on teaching for these next few days,
then to focus on you and the reason why
this holiday exists for us. AMEN.

For Students Getting Driver's Licenses

Dear God, sometimes these high-school students seem almost adult. I know they think they are. And they need to think that.

A driver's license is a rite of passage, and it's time for it now. First for a few, then by the end of the year for most of them. Please keep them in your hands, O Lord, when they are driving. Help them remember what they have learned; be with them when they are tempted to show off. Guide them as they gain the experience to become careful and competent drivers. Grant that they might pass safely on their journeys and arrive without harm at their destinations. AMEN.

For Loving the Unlovable

Look at _____, Lord.
Does he ever irritate you? Of all the students in my class, he is the least likeable.
The other children don't like him either,
and I do feel sorry for him because of that,
but I'm no better.

_____ is here to
remind us of something. He is your creation, and you love him every bit as much
as you love the rest of us. But when I avoid
him, am impatient with him, how much do
you like me then? Not very much, I suspect.

Help me remember that you love
_____. Help me remember
that I too love him as a brother in Christ.
If I can remember that I love him, then
maybe I will find him more tolerable. And
maybe that will be an example to the other
children. I will try. Please give me patience
and strength. AMEN.

Prayer for Being a Christian Example

Lord, do they know I'm a Christian? I want them to. Even though I don't speak of you openly, help me to show them that you are Ruler of my life through my love, my care, and my discipline. And help me to show them the Christ-like way to handle conflict and joy. AMEN.

Joanne Hickman

Prayer for Dealing with a Difficult Child

Lord, please let her be absent today. The class runs so smoothly when she isn't here. And I just don't feel like dealing with her today. I know she will be here, though. I guess what I really need is the wisdom to find a way to work with her. Please give me the strength to try again and the wisdom to know what to try. AMEN.

Joanne Hickman

For New Determination

Sometimes I feel like such a failure.
Sometimes I don't feel like I know what I
have been doing, or need to do. I love
teaching. I love my kids but I don't always
know how to help them. Some days are
just awful! Then, one bright special day,
one of my students gets a concept he has
wrestled with or the child who has strug-
gled to have self-control "gets it together."
Maybe, it is a day when I have seen the
regular education kids doing something
extra nice for one of my special needs children. On days like this things come
together for me and I am reminded of why
I want to be a teacher. I realize the strug-
gles I go through are worth it and actually
make me a better teacher as I see students
make progress and feel worthy and special.
When my students give me a hug, say "I
love you," or send those wonderful hand-

written notes, I know I won't give up. They are depending on me to be the best teacher I can be and to love them on the "bad" days, too. If every week I try to find ways to improve and relate my teaching to my students' lives, I have at least begun to be successful as a teacher and a person. Being a teacher is not always easy but I know God has brought me to this place and given me this responsibility because he knows I can do it! So I'll just keep plugging along doing the things I know I should, being true to myself and what I know God wants me to do. I really do believe in my students and their abilities and that they can become all God wants them to be. I feel so much better getting all this off my mind and I can feel a new determination kicking in. I will do better with God's help. I know it.

Sandra Presley

The First Day of School

Dear God, it's here, the first day of school. I am so excited. My room looks great with the new bulletin boards and I think my "teacher bear" on the door is so cute. I have some new materials and I really have a lot of good ideas from my language arts class this summer. The shelves are clean and free of clutter (that probably won't last long). I've done everything I could to make sure the year gets started off right.

Uh, Oh! I have forgotten something really important, haven't I? Lord, thank you for reminding me that the most important things I will give to my class cannot be purchased at the local school supply. There are some things I can only get from you—like patience on trying days and with students who make me want to scream sometimes, or kindness and caring for the

28

student who so desperately needs to know someone loves him, and understanding when in my mind, I really don't understand. So when I walk into my class today, help me to know I've made "heart preparations" as well as "room preparations."
AMEN.

Sandra Presley

If I Am Able

Lord, while the preacher was reading 1 Corinthians 13, I felt my heart go "flip-flop." I have heard this scripture many times but you spoke to me with a different message this time.

If I am able to teach using the most current teaching methods and have not love, I am like a clanging symbol.

If I am able to predict my students' futures, understand everything they do and have a wealth of knowledge, without love I am nothing.

Though I invest half my salary to buy things for my class without love, I gain nothing.

A teacher is patient, kind, does not boast, is not proud, is not rude or self-seeking, is not easily angered, keeps no record of wrongs, does not delight in evil but rejoices in the truth. A teacher always trusts, always hopes and perseveres.

A teacher does all these things because of the love for children. This God-given love is greater than any educational background, curriculum, or teaching method.

Thank you, God, for your Word and for speaking to my heart. Help me to love others as you have loved me. AMEN.

Sandra Presley

To See Your Face

Lord, I see your face so many times each day. At first I was surprised that you look different from the way I have pictured you in my mind. But now I've come to recognize you—in the chubby-faced, but compassionate girl who is so quick to rescue her friends from embarrassment; in the dark skinned boy with the lilting speech who humbles me with his sharing; in any of the faces looking trustingly at me as I open the day. Thank you, Lord, for showing yourself to me and help others to see your face when they look at mine. AMEN.

A Snow Day

Lord, I woke up this morning to that special light and hush that means the world outside my window is covered with snow. May I see this day as an unexpected blessing, a time to refresh myself in you. Keep me from spending too much time worrying about the work that will remain undone until school reopens. Bless the children from my school and classroom. Keep them safe. I pray especially for those children who will be home alone while their parents are at work. Be with their parents as they travel to and from their jobs. Bless the workers who are already busy clearing our streets and roads so that not too much time will be lost from those things we have come to see as important. May we all have a few moments during the day when we are aware of the beauty of your world and may that awareness bring us closer to you. AMEN.

For Children's Gifts

Dear Jesus, who gathered children into your lap and loved them, soon the children will be crowding around my desk to give me their gifts. May my acceptance of them be worthy of you. May your love flow through me to each of these little ones and may it especially warm those who are unable to bring a gift. AMEN.

Thanks for My Teachers

Dear Lord, how could I forget to say thanks for those teachers who taught me so much? Now that I am myself a teacher, I remember those who corrected my mistakes, had faith in my untried powers, encouraged me, and helped me choose this path. Thank you for those cherished memories. Help me to find a way to say a special word of gratitude to those I can still reach. Many are now beyond my reach. For them, there is still one thing I can do. In the name of Jesus, the world's greatest teacher, may I always do my best to follow both their example and his. AMEN.

In Times of Stress

O dear God, I am thankful that I have never stopped learning. Thank you for so often opening my eyes to the very things for which my heart is searching. I have been so impatient lately. Then today you led me to read about Thomas Carlyle. Carlyle had given his complete manuscript on the French Revolution to his neighbor, John Stuart Mill, to read. To their horror they learned that Mill's maid had used the manuscript to start a fire. Carlyle was in a frenzy for days. Then one day he observed a mason building a wall, laying one brick at a time. From this sight Carlyle took new courage; he could rewrite *The French Revolution* one page at a time. Thank you for letting me see this story at this time. Help me to remember it in times of stress and anxiety. AMEN.

The New Leaf

He came to my desk with quivering lip—
   The lesson was done.
"Dear Teacher, I want a new leaf," he said,
   "I have spoiled this one."
I took the old leaf, stained and blotted,
And gave him a new one, all unspotted,
   And into his sad eyes smiled:
   "Do better now, my child!"

I went to the Throne with a quivering soul—
   The old year was done.
"Dear Father, hast Thou a new leaf for me?
   I have spoiled this one."
He took the old leaf, stained and blotted,
And gave me a new one, all unspotted,
   And into my sad heart smiled:
   "Do better now, my child!"

Author Unknown

Feeling Sorry for Myself

Remember, Lord, when I was younger and first discovered I am not the center of creation? I had such big plans for that day. But from the very beginning nothing seemed to go right. The day was a complete disaster, made even worse when someone close to me told me to quit whining. Did I think I could have whatever I wanted just by wishing it?

Remember the angry prayer I began? I stormed about the injustice of my failed expectations, the unfairness of my friends and family, the constant level of disappointment, and the sorrow of being ignored by you.

That was also the first time I felt like I really got an answer in prayer. Very gently, but very insistently, you agreed with my friends. You comforted me, and slowly I became calm. I promised to never again

think of myself as the most important part
of creation.

But I have not kept that promise. Today
I am immersed in self-pity and I need to
have your gentle guidance once more.
Lead me to quiet acceptance, oh God; I am
yours. AMEN.

For Adventure
in Everyday Living

Oh God, sometimes my days seem so dull and dreary. I fall into a rut, and I don't know how to climb out. Then, when I think I've found a way out, a way to infuse my life with excitement and renewed energy, I allow my fear of change to overcome me. Help me to break out of the endless cycle of routine and predictability. Give me the courage and the faith to make each day an adventure, trusting in your steadfast love and protection. As I seek your guidance through prayer and meditation upon your word, I ask for the wisdom to make constructive changes in my life and to find new meaning and pleasure in the familiar. Knowing that you walk with me, I can face each new day with joyful anticipation. Thank you for your precious gift of life. AMEN.

A Vacation Prayer

Dear Lord, how I've waited for this vacation, and now it's finally here. Thank you, Lord, for the opportunity to take a break from my daily routine and to replenish my mind, body, and soul so that I may better serve you. Sometimes my expectations for vacations are unrealistic, and I find myself disappointed when things don't go my way. Help me not to worry about having the "perfect" vacation but to relax and enjoy every moment, whatever it may bring. I am grateful for the joys that await me—whether they be the beauty of your creation, recreation with family or friends, or peace and solitude. Watch over me and protect me as I travel, and bring me safely home again—refreshed and renewed. AMEN.

For Disappointment

Lord, I've had such a disappointment today. Something I had hoped for, dreamed of, and yes, even prayed for is just not to be. I'm hurt and I'm angry. Help me to turn loose of this bitterness. Now I see only darkness and despair. Light your lamp within me, O Lord of Light. May I see clearly through this shadow that has fallen across my life. Remind me that just as the darkness of night only hides the day for a few hours, your light shines on behind the darkness of my difficulties and disappointments. AMEN.

To Be Worthy

Dear Lord, I turn away from you even when I know better. Forgive me again and again. Help me in the same way to forgive those who are disloyal to me. Build into my character a steady, unfailing spirit of goodwill toward everyone that cannot be influenced by anything that may be done to me. Make me your worthy child. AMEN.

For Carrying on Christ's Work

Oh Christ of the loving heart, who felt tenderness and compassion for all people, inspire me to feel the same, I pray. I do not have your power to heal and restore, but your Spirit lives within me. Smile through my face, speak through my voice, use me to help the sick and suffering, the discouraged and lonely. I want to carry on your work. AMEN.

For Giving God First Place

Dear God, when I am troubled or in trouble I come to you pleading for your help, but too often when things are going well I forget about you. Help me to see your loving guidance all the time—every hour, every day. Help me to stay close to you in prosperity and success just as in difficulty and failure. Help me to put you first in my life and to hold to that standard always. AMEN.

A Christmas Shopping Prayer

Oh Christ Jesus whose birth so long ago began the traditions of today, thank you for the privilege of Christmas shopping. Help me to make even what could be a stress-filled time a time of wonder and excitement. Let me look at the Christmas decorations on city streets with the eyes of a child, to hear beyond the tinny sounds of recorded music the words of the story of your great gift to us. Make me patient in crowds, quick to smile and in some way bring a lift to the spirits of those whose work is heavier at this time. May each gift be chosen in your name and may I always give with love. AMEN.

With God

Begin the day with God:
Kneel down and say a prayer;
Lift up your heart to God's abode
And seek God's love to share.

Go through the day with God,
Whate'er your work may be;
Where'er you are—at home, abroad,
God still is near to thee.

Conclude the day with God:
Your sins to God confess;
Trust in the Lord's atoning blood,
And plead God's righteousness.

Author Unknown (adapted)

The Meaning of Prayer

A breath of prayer in the morning
Means a day of blessing sure—
A breath of prayer in the evening
Means a night of rest secure.

A breath of prayer in our weakness
Means the clasp of a mighty hand—
A breath of prayer when we're lonely
Means someone to understand.

A breath of prayer in rejoicing
Gives joy and added delight.
For they that remember God's goodness
Go singing far into the night.

There's never a year nor a season
That prayer may not bless every hour
And never a soul need be helpless
When linked with God's great power.

Author Unknown

Christian Prayers
Through the Centuries

For Joy and Gladness

Blessed are Thou, O Lord, who has nourished me from my youth up, who givest food to all flesh. Fill our hearts with joy and gladness that we, always having all sufficiency in all things, may abound to every good work in Christ Jesus our Lord, through whom to Thee be glory, honor, might, majesty and dominion, forever and ever. AMEN.

The Clementine Liturgy
First Century

For Stewardship

O Lord God Almighty, who has built Thy Church upon the foundation of the Apostles, under Christ the head cornerstone, and to this end didst endue Thy holy apostle St. Barnabas with the singular gift of the Holy Ghost; leave me not destitute, I humbly beseech Thee, of Thy manifold gifts and talents, nor yet of grace to make a right use of them always without any sordid self-ends, to Thy honour and glory; that, making a due improvement of all those gifts Thou graciously entrustest me with, I may be able to give a good account of my stewardship when the great Judge shall appear, the Lord Jesus Christ, who reigneth with Thee and the Eternal Spirit, one God, blessed forever. AMEN.

Barnabas
Second Century

Prayer for God's Help

Give perfection to beginners, O Father;
give intelligence to the little ones; give aid
to those who are running their course.
Give sorrow to the negligent; give fervor
of spirit to the lukewarm. Give to the perfect a good consummation; for the sake of
Christ Jesus our Lord. AMEN.

Irenaeus
Second Century

Morning Prayer

We give thee hearty thanks for the rest of the past night, and for the gift of a new day, with its opportunities of pleasing thee. Grant that we may so pass its hours in the perfect freedom of thy service, that at eventide we may again give thanks unto thee; through Jesus Christ our Lord. AMEN.

The Eastern Church
Third Century

For Light and Guidance

O God, our Father, who dost exhort us to pray, and who dost grant what we ask, if only, when we ask, we live a better life; hear me, who am trembling in this darkness, and stretch forth Thy hand unto me; hold forth Thy light before me; recall me from my wanderings; and, Thou being my Guide, may I be restored to myself and to Thee, through Jesus Christ. AMEN.

St. Augustine
Fourth Century

Christ, Be with Me

Christ, be with me, Christ before me,
Christ behind me,
Christ in me, Christ beneath me, Christ
above me,
Christ on my right, Christ on my left.
Christ when I lie, Christ when I sit, Christ
when I arise,
Christ in the heart of every one who
thinks of me,
Christ in the mouth of every one who
speaks of me,
Christ in every eye that sees me.
Christ in every ear that hears me.
  Salvation is of the Lord,
  Salvation is of the Lord
  Salvation is of the Christ,
  May your salvation, O Lord, be ever
    with us.

St. Patrick
Fifth Century

Daily Prayer of Thomas Aquinas

Grant me, I beseech Thee, O merciful God, prudently to study, rightly to understand, and perfectly to fulfill that which is pleasing to Thee, to the praise and glory of Thy name.

Thou, O Christ, art the King of glory; Thou art the everlasting Son of the Father. AMEN.

Thomas Aquinas
Thirteenth Century

Praising God of Many Names

O burning Mountain, O chosen Sun,
O perfect Moon, O fathomless Well,
O unattainable Height, O Clearness
    beyond Measure,
O Wisdom without end, O Mercy without
    limit,
O Strength beyond resistance, O Crown
    beyond all majesty:
The humblest thing you created sings your
    praise. AMEN.

Mechtil of Magdelburg
Germany, Thirteenth Century

For Thy Spirit

The prayers I make will then be sweet
    indeed,
If Thou the spirit give by which I pray;
My unassisted heart is barren clay,
That of its native self can nothing feed;
Of good and pious works Thou art the seed
That quickens only where Thou say'st it may.
Unless Thou show to us Thy own true way,
No man can find it! Father! Thou must lead;
Do Thou then breathe those thoughts into
    my mind
By which such virtue may in me be bred
That in Thy holy footsteps I may tread;
The fetters of my tongue do Thou unbind,
That I may have the power to sing to Thee,
And sound Thy praises everlastingly!
AMEN.

Michelangelo
Fifteenth Century

Prayer for Friends

Almighty, everlasting God, have mercy on Thy servants our friends. Keep them continually under Thy protection, and direct them according to Thy gracious favour in the way of everlasting salvation; that they may desire such things as please Thee, and with all their strength perform the same. And forasmuch as they trust in Thy mercy, vouchsafe, O Lord, graciously to assist them with Thy heavenly help, that they may ever diligently serve Thee, and by no temptations be separated from Thee; through Jesus Christ our Lord. AMEN.

Thomas à Kempis
Fifteenth Century

The Sufficiency of God

God, of your goodness give me yourself;
for you are sufficient for me. I cannot prop-
erly ask anything less, to be worthy of you.
If I were to ask less I should always be in
want. In you alone do I have all. AMEN.

Juliane of Norwich
Fifteenth Century

For Overcoming Adversity

Lord, we pray not for tranquility,
   nor that our tribulations may cease;
we pray for thy spirit and thy love,
   that thou grant us strength and
   grace to overcome adversity;
      through Jesus Christ. AMEN.

Girolamo Savonarola
Fifteenth Century

Give Me Grace

Give me thy grace, good Lord,
To set the world at nought,
To set my mind fast on thee.
And not to hang upon the blast of men's
    mouths.
To be content to be solitary,
Not to long for worldly company,
Little and little utterly to cast off the world,
And rid my mind of all the business thereof.
Gladly to be thinking of God,
Piteously to call for his help,
To lean upon the comfort of God,
Busily to labor to love him.

Thomas More
Sixteenth Century

Morning Prayer

We give thanks unto thee, heavenly Father, through Jesus Christ thy dear Son, that thou hast protected us through the night from all danger and harm; and we beseech thee to preserve and keep us, this day also, from all sin and evil; that in all our thoughts, words, and deeds, we may serve and please thee. Into thy hands we commend our bodies and souls, and all that is ours. Let thy holy angel have charge concerning us that the wicked one have no power over us. AMEN.

Martin Luther
Sixteenth Century

For Peace

In these our days so perilous,
Lord, peace in mercy send us;
No God but thee can fight for us,
No God but thee defend us;
    Thou our only God and Savior.

Martin Luther

For Imitation of Christ

Almighty God, inasmuch as thou hast been pleased to set before us an example of every perfection in thine only-begotten Son, grant that we may study to form ourselves in imitation of him. May we follow not only what he has prescribed, but also what he performed, that we may truly prove ourselves to be his members, and thus confirm our adoption. May we so proceed in the whole course of our life that we may at length be gathered into that blessed rest which the same, thine only-begotten Son, hath obtained for us by his own blood. AMEN.

John Calvin
Sixteenth Century

Good Works

Grant, almighty God, since thou art pleased kindly to invite us to thyself, and have consecrated thy Word for our salvation, that we may willingly, and from the heart, obey thee, and become teachable. May we be so planted in the courts of thine house, that we may grow and flourish, and that fruit may appear through the whole course of our life, until we shall at length enjoy that blessed life which is laid up for us in heaven, through Christ our Lord. AMEN.

John Calvin
Sixteenth Century

Reliance on God

O Lord,
never suffer us to think
that we can stand by ourselves,
and not need thee.

John Donne
Seventeenth Century

Prayer for the Soul

Eternal and most glorious God, suffer me not so to undervalue myself as to give away my soul, Thy soul, Thy dead and precious soul, for nothing; and all the world is nothing, if the soul must be given for it. Preserve therefore, my soul, O Lord, because it belongs to Thee, and preserve my body because it belongs to my soul. Thou alone dost steer my boat through all its voyage, but hast a more special care of it, when it comes to a narrow current, or to a dangerous fall of waters. Thou hast a care of the preservation of my body in all the ways of my life; but, in the straits of death, open Thine eyes wider, and enlarge Thy Providence towards me so far that no illness or agony may shake and benumb the soul. Do Thou so make my bed in all my sickness that, being used to Thy hand, I may be content with any bed of Thy making. AMEN.

John Donne

Fix Then Our Steps

Fix Thou our steps, O Lord, that we stagger not at the uneven motions of the world, but steadily go on to our glorious home, neither censuring our journey by the weather we meet with, nor turning out of the way for anything that befalls us.

John Wesley
Eighteenth Century

In Thy Service

Thou art never weary, O Lord, of doing us good. Let us never be weary of doing thee service. But, as thou hast pleasure in the prosperity of thy servants, so let us take pleasure in the service of our Lord, and abound in thy work, and in thy love and praise evermore. O fill up all that is wanting, reform whatever is amiss in us, perfect the thing that concerneth us. Let the witness of thy pardoning love ever abide in all our hearts.

John Wesley
Eighteenth Century

For the Spirit's Liberty

Deliver me, O God, from too intense an application to even necessary business. I know the narrowness of my heart and that an eager attention to earthly things leaves it no room for the things of heaven. Teach me to go through all my employments with so truly disengaged a heart that I may still see thee in all things, and that I may never impair that liberty of spirit which is necessary for the love of thee.

John Wesley
Eighteenth Century

For a Lively Spirit

Deliver me, O God, from a slothful mind, from all lukewarmness and all dejection of spirit. I know these cannot but deaden my life to thee; mercifully free my heart from them, and give me a lively, zealous, active and cheerful spirit that I may vigorously perform whatever thou commandest and be ever ardent to obey in all things thy holy love.

John Wesley
Eighteenth Century

Thanks for the Eucharist

Whither, O my God, should we wander if left to ourselves? Where should we fix our hearts if not directed by thee?

Thou didst send forth thy Holy Spirit to guide and comfort us, and give thyself in the Holy Eucharist to feed and nourish our hungry souls with that sacramental food.

Still thou art really present to us in that holy mystery of love; hence we offer up our devotions in it with our utmost reverence, wonder, and love.

John Wesley
Eighteenth Century

For Holiness

Cure us, O thou great Physician of souls, of all our sinful distempers.

Cure us of this intermitting piety, and fix it into an even and a constant holiness.

Oh, make us use religion as our regular diet and not only as a medicine in necessity.

Make us enter into a course of hearty repentance and practice virtue as our daily exercise.

So shall our souls be endued with perfect health and disposed for a long, even for an everlasting, life.

John Wesley
Eighteenth Century

Jesus, Lover Of My Soul

Jesus, lover of my soul,
Let me to thy bosom fly,
While the nearer waters roll,
While the tempest still is high:
Hide me, O my Savior, hide,
Till the storm of life is past;
Safe into the haven guide;
O receive my soul at last!

Charles Wesley
Eighteenth Century

Prayer

Only, O Lord, in Thy dear love
Fit us for perfect rest above:
And help us this and every day,
To live more nearly as we pray.

John Keble
Nineteenth Century

For Peace

O Lord, support us all the day long of
this troublous life, until the shadows
lengthen, and the evening comes, and the
busy world is hushed, and the fever of life
is over, and our work is done. Then, in
Thy great mercy, grant us a safe lodging,
and a holy rest, and peace at the last;
through Jesus Christ our Lord. AMEN.

John Henry Newman
Nineteenth Century

Stay With Me

Stay with me, and then I shall begin to shine as thou shinest: so to shine as to be a light to others. The light, O Jesus, will be all from thee. None of it will be mine. No merit to me. It will be thou who shinest through me upon others. O let me thus praise thee, in the way which thou dost love best, by shining on all those around me. Give light to them as well as to me; light them with me, through me. Teach me to show forth thy praise, thy truth, thy will. Make me preach thee without preaching—not by words, but by my example and by the catching force, the sympathetic influence, of what I do—by my visible resemblance to thy saints, and the evident fulness of the love which my heart bears to thee.

John Henry Newman
Nineteenth Century

Ever a Child

Thou, O my God, art ever new, though
thou art the most ancient—thou alone art
the floor for eternity. I am to live for ever,
not for a time—and I have no power over
my being; I cannot destroy myself, even
though I were so wicked as to wish to do
so. I must live on, with intellect and con-
sciousness for ever, in spite of myself.
Without thee eternity would be another
name for eternal misery. In thee alone
have I that which can stay me up for ever:
thou alone art the food of my soul. Thou
alone art inexhaustible, and ever offerest
to me something new to know, something
new to love . . . and so on for eternity I
shall ever be a little child beginning to be
taught the rudiments of thy infinite divine
nature. For thou art thyself the seat and
centre of all good, and the only substance
in this universe of shadows, and the

heaven in which blessed spirits live and
rejoice—AMEN.

John Henry Newman
Nineteenth Century

To the Holy Spirit

As the wind is thy symbol
so forward our goings.
As the dove
so launch us heavenwards.
As water
so purify our spirits.
As a cloud
so abate our temptations.
As dew
so revive our languor.
As fire
so purge out our dross.

Christina Rossetti
Nineteenth Century

Thy Greatness

God in Heaven, let me really feel my
nothingness, not in order to despair over
it, but in order to feel the more powerfully
the greatness of Thy goodness.

Søren Kierkegaard
Nineteenth Century

Thou Hast Loved Us First

Father in Heaven! Thou hast loved us first, help us never to forget that Thou art love so that this sure conviction might triumph in our hearts over the seduction of the world, over the inquietude of the soul, over the anxiety for the future, over the fright of the past, over the distress of the moment. But grant also that this conviction might discipline our soul so that our heart might remain faithful and sincere in the love which we bear to all those whom Thou hast commanded us to love as we love ourselves.

Søren Kierkegaard
Nineteenth Century

Waking

Father in Heaven! When the thought of Thee wakes in our hearts let it not awaken like a frightened bird that flies about in dismay, but like a child waking from its sleep with a heavenly smile.

Søren Kierkegaard
Nineteenth Century

For Illumination

Open wide the window of our spirits, O
Lord, and fill us full of light; open wide the
door of our hearts, that we may receive
and entertain thee with all our powers of
adoration and love. AMEN.

Christina Rossetti
Nineteenth Century

My Heart

Father, into thy hands I give the heart
Which left thee but to learn how good
thou art.

George Macdonald
Twentieth Century

A Fool I Bring

When I look back upon my life nigh spent,
Nigh spent, although the stream as yet
    flows on,
I more of follies than of sins repent,
Less for offence than love's shortcomings
    moan.
With self, O Father, leave me not alone—
Leave not with the beguiler the beguiled;
Besmirched and ragged, Lord, take back
    thine own;
A fool I bring thee to be made a child.

George Macdonald
Twentieth Century

In Praise of the Night

O Lord, we praise Thee for our sister, the Night, who folds all the tired folk of the earth in her comfortable robe of darkness and gives them sleep. Release now the strained limbs of toil and smooth the brow of care. Grant us the refreshing draught of forgetfulness, that we may rise in the morning with a smile on our face. Comfort and ease those who toss wakeful on a bed of pain, or those whose aching nerves crave sleep and find it not. Save them from evil or despondent thoughts in the long darkness, and teach them so to lean on Thy all-pervading life and love, that their souls may grow tranquil and their bodies, too, may rest. And now, through Thee we send Good Night to all our brothers and sisters near and far, and pray for peace upon all the earth. AMEN.

Walter Rauschenbusch
Twentieth Century

For the Spirit of Truth

From the cowardice that dares not face
   new truth,
from the laziness that is contented with
   half-truth,
from the arrogance that thinks it knows all
   truth,
Good Lord, deliver me. AMEN.

Prayer from Kenya

A Refuge Amid Distraction

Like an ant on a stick both ends of which
   are burning,
   I go to and fro without knowing what to
   do,
     and in great despair.
Like the inescapable shadow that follows
   me,
   the dead weight of sin haunts me.
Graciously look upon me.
Thy love is my refuge. AMEN.

Traditional
India

For the Unity of Christ's Body

Help each of us, gracious God,
   to live in such magnanimity and restraint
that the Head of the church may never have
cause to say to any one of us,
   "This is my body, broken by you."
AMEN.

Chinese Prayer

For a New Day

We give you hearty thanks for the rest of
    the past night
        and for the gift of a new day, with its
        opportunities of pleasing you.
Grant that we may so pass its hours in the
    perfect freedom
        of your service,
    that at eventide we may again give
        thanks unto you. AMEN.

Eastern Orthodox Prayer

For Protection at Night

Dear Jesus, as a hen covers her chicks with her wings to keep them safe, do thou this night protect us under your golden wings. AMEN.

Traditional
India

For a Peaceful Night

O God, you have let me pass the day in
    peace;
let me pass the night in peace, O Lord who
    has no Lord.
There is no strength but in you. You alone
    have no obligation.
Under your hand I pass the night.
You are my Mother and my Father. AMEN.

Traditional prayer of the Boran people

For True Life

Govern all by thy wisdom, O Lord,
    so that my soul may always be serving thee
      as thou dost will,
      and not as I may choose.
Do not punish me, I beseech thee,
    by granting that which I wish or ask,
      if it offend thy love, which would
      always live in me.
Let me die to myself, that I may serve thee;
let me live to thee, who in thyself art the
true life. AMEN

Teresa of Avila
Spain
Sixteenth Century

A Daily Prayer

O God, let this be my prayer every day.
Keep me from thinking any critical
thought. Keep me from blaming others for
anything. Keep me from being resentful.
Keep me from saying or thinking any hurt-
ful thing about anyone. Help me today and
every day to think good and do good
regardless of what anyone else may say or
do. Spirit of all power and goodness, quiet
my mind. Help me to be still enough to
hear your voice. Help me to stop worrying
and fretting. Help me to stop rebelling
against circumstances. Help me to be like
Jesus. AMEN.

For God's Help in Relationships

All wise and loving God, you know how blind I can be to my own faults and how quick I sometimes am to see the faults of others. Clear my eyes, I pray, so that I can see both myself and others as we truly are. Help me to practice your great commandments to love you with all my being and to love others as myself. I can't do it alone, but with your help I can. Thank you for your unfailing love. AMEN.